LIZZO

BREAKOUT ARTIST

LAKITA WILSON

LERNER PUBLICATIONS ◆ MINNEAPOLIS

To all the girls who live out loud . . . keep going.

Lerner Publications Company
An imprint of Lerner Publishing Group, Inc.
241 First Avenue North
Minneapolis, MN 55401 USA

For reading levels and more information, look up this title at www.lernerbooks.com.

Image credits: Kevin Mazur/AMA2019/dcp/Getty Images, pp. 2, 8; Emma McIntyre/dcp/Getty Images, p. 6; Tim Mosenfelder/Getty Images, pp. 9, 23; Gareth Cattermole/Getty Images, p. 10; Annabel Staff/ Redferns/Getty Images, p. 11; Shareif Ziyadat/WireImage/Getty Images, p. 12; ANGELA WEISS/AFP/ Getty Images, p. 13; Gary Wolstenholme/Redferns/Getty Images, p. 14; Richard E. Aaron/Redferns/ Getty Images, p. 15; Steve Skjold/Shutterstock.com, p. 16; Kevin Mazur/The Recording Academy/Getty Images, p. 17; John Shearer/Getty Images, p. 18; PH888/Shutterstock.com, p. 19; Frazer Harrison/ Spotify/Getty Images, p. 20; Michael Boardman/WireImage/Getty Images, p. 21; VALERIE MACON/AFP/ Getty Images, p. 22; Charley Gallay/Pandora/Getty Images, p. 24; John Lamparski/Getty Images, p. 25; Timothy Norris/Coachella/Getty Images, p. 26; Kevin Winter/MTV/Getty Images, p. 27; Kevin Winter/ Getty Images, p. 28; Frederick M. Brown/BET/Getty Images, p. 29; Franziska Krug/Getty Images, p. 31; David Crotty/Patrick McMullan/Getty Images, p. 32; Francis Specker/CBS/Getty Images, p. 33; Steve Granitz/WireImage/Getty Images, pp. 34, 35; Matt Jelonek/Wire Image/Getty Images, p. 36; Frederic Legrand—COMEO/Shutterstock.com, p. 37; Rich Fury/Coachella/Getty Images, p. 38. Cover image: Kevin Mazur/AMA2019/dcp/Getty Images.

Main body text set in Rotis Serif Std 55 Regular. Typeface provided by Adobe Systems.

Editor: Jordyn Taylor

Library of Congress Cataloging-in-Publication Data

Names: Wilson, Lakita, author.
Title: Lizzo : breakout artist / Lakita Wilson.
Description: Minneapolis : Lerner Publications, 2021 | Series: Gateway biographies | Includes bibliographical references and index. | Audience: Ages 9–14 | Audience: Grades 4–6 | Summary: "Lizzo started singing and rapping with musical groups in her hometowns of Houston and Minneapolis. With her fun lyrics, danceable beats, and positive message, she's become one of the biggest solo musicians in the world"– Provided by publisher.
Identifiers: LCCN 2020003615 (print) | LCCN 2020003616 (ebook) | ISBN 9781541596788 (library binding) | ISBN 9781728413518 (paperback) | ISBN 9781728400297 (ebook)
Subjects: LCSH: Lizzo, 1988-–Juvenile literature. | Singers–United States–Biography–Juvenile literature. | Rap musicians–United States–Biography–Juvenile literature. | CYAC: Lizzo, 1988- | Singers–United States–Biography. | Rap musicians–United States–Biography.
Classification: LCC ML3930.L579 W55 2020 (print) | LCC ML3930.L579 (ebook) | DDC 782.421649092 [B]–dc23

LC record available at https://lccn.loc.gov/2020003615
LC ebook record available at https://lccn.loc.gov/2020003616

Manufactured in the United States of America
1-47785-48225-4/29/2020

CONTENTS

Lizzo fans love her style at awards shows. She carried this tiny purse to the 2019 American Music Awards.

On November 24, 2019, Lizzo stepped onto the American Music Awards (AMAs) carpet wearing long, dangling earrings; hair swooped up into a glamorous high ponytail; and a coral minidress. Her shoulder-bearing dress was beautiful, but it was her tiny purse that stole the show. "It's custom—there's only three in the world!" Lizzo exclaimed, holding up the little white Valentino bag as cameras flashed. Instantly, images of Lizzo and her bag were all over social media. Millions of fans from around the world hit the Like button more than a million times. Celebrities filled her social media feeds with comments of approval under Lizzo's posts.

Months earlier, Lizzo had learned that she'd been nominated for three major awards at the AMAs: New Artist of the Year, Favorite Female Artist: Soul/R&B, and Favorite Song: Soul/R&B for her single "Juice." And Lizzo was proud of her music. She welcomed the recognition.

Lizzo's performance at the AMAs brought the audience to its feet.

That evening Lizzo gave the audience a taste of her musical talents by performing her newest single, "Jerome," in a floor-length raspberry-colored gown. She stood on a circular platform that slowly spun her around like a ballerina in a music box as she crooned about being too valuable to let an unworthy man bring her down. Lizzo hit the last note and sank to her knees as the audience rose for a standing ovation.

Many people in the room assumed Lizzo was a brand-new musical artist. But Lizzo had been singing for quite some time. She had already released two albums that went mostly unnoticed before shooting to stardom with her hit song "Truth Hurts."

"Truth Hurts" was released in 2017. But the single became popular in 2018 when it was featured in the Netflix movie *Someone Great*. After that, streams of the song quadrupled. Lizzo's management team rereleased the song on her 2019 album *Cuz I Love You*, and soon Lizzo's upbeat music was on playlists all over the world.

Lizzo didn't win any awards that night, but she didn't stop smiling. For eight years, Lizzo had experienced the ups and downs of being a music artist. She told *People* magazine in June 2019 that "the song that made me want to quit is the song that everyone's falling in love with me for, which is such a testament to journeys. Your darkest day turns into your brightest triumph."

As she headed to the AMAs after-party, she was already living her dream of making music for the world and performing on large stages. A week earlier, she'd gotten the news that she'd been nominated for a record-breaking eight Grammy Awards. And just a few weeks after the Grammy nominations, Lizzo learned she'd been named 2019's Entertainer of the Year by *Time* magazine and the Associated Press.

Lizzo onstage during her sold-out Cuz I Love You tour

But for Lizzo, her biggest triumph is still out there, waiting to make its grand appearance. As she sees it, her award wins are only the beginning.

Born to Sing

Lizzo was born Melissa Viviane Jefferson on April 27, 1988, in Detroit, Michigan. She was the youngest in a family of three siblings including herself; her older sister, Vanessa; and her older brother, Mikey. A lot of music was played in the Jefferson house, but not the kind of music you might find on a Lizzo album. "I grew up with a lot of gospel music," Lizzo says. Her family was religious and believed that secular, or nonreligious, music was inappropriate.

While in Detroit, Lizzo struggled with her appearance. She thought her skin was too dark, her hair

Lizzo first started singing as a young child.

too curly, and her body too large. When Lizzo looked in the mirror, she wanted to be something other than the person she saw staring back at her. She was even insecure about her voice. In 2019, while appearing on the morning radio show the *Breakfast Club*, Lizzo revealed that for three years of her childhood, she didn't talk at all because she was afraid her voice annoyed people.

Lizzo was always interested in music. She sang in the church choir and learned how to perform in front of an audience. At church she learned about staying true to herself, and that wisdom has stuck with her. Lizzo says, "I had a woman say . . . to me once . . . 'You're going to try to lose weight but it's not going to happen because when you grow up you're going to be a celebrity and

Lizzo didn't always have the confidence to sing in front of large crowds.

you're going to help girls love themselves, looking the way that they look.'"

When Lizzo was nine, her family moved from Detroit to Houston, Texas. Then Lizzo discovered hip-hop and a very special artist that she could relate to—another brown-skinned girl named Melissa.

In the 1990s, Missy "Misdemeanor" Elliott was making a name for herself as a rap and R&B star. Suddenly, Lizzo's love for playing flute in her middle school band *and* performing in a rap group with her friends seemed normal. Missy didn't fit into one simple box. And Lizzo didn't have to either.

Lizzo learned a lot about music by following her idol, Missy Elliott.

FLUTIST

Lizzo played the flute in elementary school and middle school. In high school, she played the piccolo in her school's marching band. Lizzo's flute skills earned her a college scholarship to the University of Houston.

Lizzo still plays the flute, and she loves her flute so much that she named it Sasha Flute after Beyoncé's alter ego, Sasha Fierce. In 2019 Lizzo got a second, blue flute that she named Blew Ivy, a play on the name of Beyoncé's daughter, Blue Ivy Carter. Both are custom concert flutes made by Muramatsu, Japan's oldest flute company.

Lizzo plays the flute at most of her performances.

Becoming Lizzo

Lizzo worked hard in both band and in her classes. She was a good student throughout middle school and high school. By the time she enrolled at the University of Houston, she planned to join a symphony ensemble one day. However, money became tight for Lizzo just before her junior year of college. Lizzo left the University of Houston and moved to Minnesota for a fresh start.

In Minnesota, Lizzo spent six years working on her music. Things weren't easy for her in her new home state. She slept on the floor of rehearsal studios when she didn't have a place to live. She ate at friends' houses for dinner when there wasn't enough money for groceries. And her father died when she was twenty-one years old.

Making it big in the music industry meant facing plenty of struggles and teaching herself how to overcome them. But one of

Lizzo honed her talent by spending years onstage in front of an audience.

Lizzo's biggest challenges was her confidence. She still didn't have a lot of confidence about her body, and she worried a great deal about what others thought of her.

During her years in Minnesota, Lizzo attempted to hide in the background. She sang as a background vocalist because she didn't feel comfortable enough singing lead or solo. Lizzo often found herself in groups with women she thought were prettier, cooler, or more interesting than she was. She would put them on a pedestal, thinking they deserved the spotlight more than she did.

Prince was one of Minnesota's greatest musicians. Many artists looked up to him, including Lizzo.

The first girl band Lizzo joined was a pop group named the Chalice. Her next group, GRRRL PRTY, rapped and sang. They were known for putting on thrilling shows. Minnesota-based artist Prince noticed GRRRL PRTY's talent and wild onstage antics and invited them to record a song, "Boytrouble." He even asked them

Paisley Park is where Prince recorded many songs, including "Boytrouble."

to play a show at Paisley Park, his private estate and music production complex.

Producing a song with Prince made Lizzo feel validated, as if someone cared about her music. She also earned her first big check in the music industry. Yet Lizzo still had just one fear to get over: she needed to face her nervousness over being in the spotlight. If Lizzo was going to make a name for herself, she would have to go solo.

One day in 2014, Lizzo agreed to participate in an interview for the What's Underneath project, a series of online videos in which people share sensitive or difficult parts of their life stories. She talked about her journey to loving her body. This was Lizzo's *aha* moment. When the interviewer asked her favorite thing about herself, Lizzo said that she loved her skin.

That moment inspired her to write a song called "My Skin." She begins the song by telling her listeners that learning to love yourself is a journey. Lizzo continued celebrating her skin by wearing bodysuits and other clothing choices that showed off her beautiful brown complexion.

Lizzo's onstage style is fun and colorful.

Learning to appreciate her skin led Lizzo to take a look at another aspect of her appearance—her hair. As a teenager, Lizzo hid her natural hair under rough synthetic wigs. Now when Lizzo isn't performing, she celebrates her naturally bouncy curls by wearing them swept up on her head or around her face like a crown. Onstage, Lizzo still wears colorful waist-length wigs—but Lizzo's hair and makeup squad handles her natural hair with care first, tucking her curls under wig caps so the curls won't get damaged. Then the team adds custom hairpieces that celebrate African

American hair textures and curl patterns. For Lizzo, loving herself just as she is and identifying what she loves most about her appearance comes much more naturally these days.

Big Grrrl Small World

With her new confidence, Lizzo was finally ready to move forward on a solo project. Her first solo album, *Lizzobangers*, started with a tweet. "I wish I could afford a Lazerbeak beat," she tweeted. Lazerbeak is a popular music producer from Minnesota. At the time, it seemed to Lizzo that Lazerbeak wouldn't be willing to work with an up-and-coming singer like her. But to her surprise, the producer responded to her tweet and offered to work with her.

In the studio, Lizzo showed off her musical talents and Lazerbeak stayed and worked with her on an entire album. In 2013 Lizzo released *Lizzobangers*.

Lizzobangers was full of catchy, upbeat songs. Determined to stay true to herself, Lizzo avoided bragging about riches and fame as some other rappers do. Instead, she used her real-life experiences to describe the life of an indie artist to her listeners. Lizzo rapped about not having a car and not making a lot of money yet. She honored her ancestors with songs like "Bloodlines." She also looked to the future with songs like "Bus Passes and Happy Meals," which confidently mapped out her plans to take over the music industry.

In 2015 Lizzo released a second album, *Big Grrrl Small World*. She brought in her former bandmates from GRRRL PRTY and the Chalice to add extra fun to songs like "Batches and Cookies," where she talks about being in love—with herself. Over futuristic beats and dramatic melodies, Lizzo searches for someone who can complete her, only to realize her happiness comes from within.

Lizzo's producer Ricky Reed encouraged her to experiment with her sound and style on her debut album.

After forging her way as an artist in Minnesota, Lizzo felt ready to move to a city known for its entertainment scene—Los Angeles. In LA, Lizzo met with Ricky Reed, a producer who worked with artists Kesha, Pitbull, and Meghan Trainor. Reed produced *Coconut Oil*, Lizzo's second EP (an extended play recording, shorter than a full-length album but longer than a single). While working on the album, Ricky Reed asked her about her singing voice. Before that, Lizzo primarily rapped. But Reed was working with her on the beat for a gospel song called "Worship." He wanted to hear if she could pull off the vocals.

Lizzo told Reed she sang a little growing up but wasn't confident she could hit the notes. But once Lizzo began singing, she blew Reed away. In an article for *Teen Vogue*, Reed claimed Lizzo sounded like famous soul singers

Aretha Franklin and Chaka Khan. When Reed left the studio that day, he immediately called his manager and told him, "We need Lizzo. The *world* needs Lizzo."

Ricky Reed signed Lizzo to Atlantic Records in 2016. In late 2016, *Coconut Oil* was released, and one of her songs was featured in the movie *Barbershop: The Next Cut.* Lizzo also started hosting *Wonderland*, MTV's first live music show in twenty years.

After signing with Atlantic Records, Lizzo immediately went to work on a new single. She released "Truth Hurts" on September 19, 2017. Its reception was modest at best. That day Lizzo almost quit the music industry entirely. She told *Elle* magazine that she felt as if she was throwing music into the world and not even making a splash. Lizzo spent lots of time in her room crying.

Despite her success, Lizzo still had to learn how to deal with setbacks.

SOMEONE GREAT

Actors DeWanda Wise (*middle*) and Gina Rodriguez (*right*) danced to "Truth Hurts" in a Netflix movie, making the song gain instant popularity.

She texted her producer to admit how down she felt about her solo career and how she felt as if no one cared. Her producer came to her apartment to console her. He told her, "Even if [your] music [doesn't] feel important to the world, it [is] important to the two of [us]."

This helped Lizzo continue as an artist. She didn't know it then, but her decision to keep going would pay off in a big way just two years later.

In 2019 something amazing happened. When "Truth Hurts" came out in September 2017, people barely listened. But when it was added to the Netflix romantic comedy *Someone Great*, the song took off. In the film, two actors, Gina Rodriguez and DeWanda Wise, dance to "Truth Hurts" while singing along to the lyrics. It was these song lyrics that caught the attention of movie watchers everywhere. All of a sudden, people were searching for Lizzo's songs on all the popular music streaming services.

On the social media platform TikTok, people began making videos showing themselves lip-syncing to the opening line of the song. Many of those videos went viral. Atlantic Records decided to add "Truth Hurts" to the deluxe edition of Lizzo's upcoming third studio album, *Cuz I Love You*.

In 2018, as Lizzo set out to begin working on her first major studio album, she stood in the Atlantic Records office looking at a picture of Aretha Franklin hanging on the wall. Lizzo wanted to create a collection of songs like the Queen of Soul's album *I Never Loved a Man the Way I Love You*—an album that defined Franklin's career. Just as she'd done

Lizzo wanted to make music that left a lasting impression, like other great artists before her.

with her last two albums, Lizzo reflected on her own struggles to help her create music.

Depression was something Lizzo had dealt with her entire life. But in the summer of 2018, her mood took a serious dip. She cried a lot. She was constantly sick. Onstage, she told her audience, "Y'all, I'm not going to lie. I'm not feeling myself."

Lizzo decided to try therapy. She still struggled with confidence, self-love, and accepting herself inside and out. Regular visits with her therapist helped Lizzo understand that working on her confidence and self-love wouldn't be easy. It would be a struggle for the rest of her life. Her days in therapy helped shape her new album too. Every song on *Cuz I Love You* was inspired by the summer she attended therapy. When *Cuz I Love You* came out on April 17, 2019, it was full of love. Lizzo stayed true to loving herself—no matter what.

Better in Color

Summer 2019 was set to be a big performance season for Lizzo—the first time many new fans would see her perform live. Lizzo worked closely with her creative director, Quinn Wilson, to pull off the right looks for each performance. Wilson also began suggesting ideas for videos, social media content, and album covers.

Thanks to Wilson's unique vision, Lizzo's Coachella performance alongside rapper Childish Gambino and singer Janelle Monae had a fun, wild vibe. Her appearances at red carpet events and morning talk shows such as the *Today Show* saw Lizzo sporting colorful looks that sometimes went against fashion norms. Together, Wilson and Lizzo made sure Lizzo made a splash wherever she went.

Lizzo started on small stages, but her fame propelled her to perform for national audiences, such as her appearance on the *Today Show* in 2019.

Lizzo's spectacular costumes made her stand out from other performers at Coachella in 2019.

On June 23, 2019, Lizzo gave her first national performance on the televised MTV Movie and TV Awards. Dressed in a long, gathered choir robe, Lizzo stood in one spot on the large stage and shyly sang into the microphone. As the audience leaned forward, straining to hear her better, a woman could be seen on the teleprompter giving instructions to her backup dancers, who were still gathered backstage. She told them to remove their choir robes.

They looked confused, but the woman repeated her instructions. So the backup dancers quickly pulled at their robes, letting them slide to the floor before rushing onto the stage.

As the backup dancers rushed up in overalls, cropped tees, stretchy pants, and other streetwear, Lizzo tore off her own robe, throwing it into the audience and revealing a denim top and matching denim pants with laces going up the sides. The pace of the music picked up, and the audience responded. Lizzo began to reveal her true onstage personality. As the backup dancers bounced, flipped, and danced across the stage in sync, Lizzo held up the center, her voice rising and holding long notes as she pulled off intricate dance steps.

Lizzo's denim outfit was a hit with fans at the 2019 MTV Movie and TV Awards.

By the time Lizzo paused the dance routine to direct her background singers in an impromptu *Sister Act*-style choir rehearsal, the audience members were on their feet, clapping, cheering, and following Lizzo's instructions to sing "La-la-la-la-la" whenever Lizzo demanded during the electrifying performance. It was a show that no one in attendance would soon forget.

The 2019 MTV Movie and TV Awards wasn't the only time Lizzo and her crew did the unexpected. Backstage at the 2019 BET Awards, Lizzo and her backup dancers mysteriously huddled together and chanted "We gettin' married!" Many of her fans were confused. When did Lizzo have time to fall in love? Who was the lucky person?

When Lizzo hit the stage, her background dancers positioned themselves around the base of a larger-than-life wedding cake while Lizzo stood on top as the fancy centerpiece. Wearing all white, Lizzo flipped the long veil covering her face to reveal large, sparkling, black sunshades.

Ripping the white tulle skirt from her waist, Lizzo jumped from the cake to the stage in a white embroidered bodysuit and began singing "Truth Hurts." Midway through the song, Lizzo turned her back to the audience to show off her dancing skills. When she faced the audience again, Sasha Flute was in her hands and ready for her solo. Without missing a beat, Lizzo placed Sasha Flute to her lips and played the melody of "Truth Hurts." The audience went wild.

Lizzo plays the "Truth Hurts" melody on Sasha Flute at the 2019 BET Awards.

FLUTE FITNESS

To play her flute well, Lizzo had to learn to practice good posture, coordination, and dexterity. She also needed good lung capacity—the ability to hold a lot of air in her lungs at once. At one of her concerts, Lizzo decided to show off her flute skills with a little something extra. Playing her flute flawlessly, Lizzo surprised the audience by "hitting the shoot"—or doing a dance made popular by BlocBoy JB's viral video "Shoot." Dancing and playing the flute at the same time takes a lot of physical training. With her "flute-and-shoot" performance, Lizzo showed that she can play with the best of them!

After the BET performance, Lizzo tweeted about the reason she chose to perform as a bride. It had nothing to do with finding the perfect partner. "There's nothing I'd rather see than black girls falling in love with themselves on T.V.," she tweeted. "Big girls—you are IT. YOU ARE ALWAYS the bride in a marriage of SELF-LOVE!"

Lizzo Style

Lizzo didn't spend her entire summer flexing her vocal cords and wowing audiences with performances that kept them on their toes. In June 2019, Lizzo was named one of five Global Citizens for the beauty brand Urban Decay. The brand wanted celebrities who could encourage their customers to be individuals. Urban Decay chose Lizzo to work on their Pretty Different campaign because she didn't buy into typical beauty standards. Lizzo's unique style and originality would help Urban Decay send the right message about individuality to its customers.

Urban Decay used their bright colors to give Lizzo memorable and unique makeup looks.

In Urban Decay's first video campaign, while everyone else wore identical pink sweat suits and sprayed-on makeup, Lizzo and her fellow beauty ambassadors crashed the party with unique outfits and bold makeup looks. Ripping through the crowd of sameness, Lizzo and friends showed off their original looks while words like *Pretty Bold, Pretty Wild,* and *Pretty Uniq*ue flashed across the screen. With the brand ambassadors leading the way, the pink sweat suit crew followed after them, ripping off their sweatshirts and revealing their own unique styles.

Lizzo changed her outfit three times at the 2019 Grammy Awards.

Lizzo's music was so hot in 2019 that superstars rushed to work on songs with her. She worked with artists like DaBaby and Ariana Grande. She went on to sell out two tours, and then, on November 20, 2019, the Recording Academy announced Lizzo was nominated for eight Grammy Awards.

On the night of the 62nd Grammy Awards, Lizzo decided to represent the past, present, and future. Arriving at the Staples Center in Los Angeles, Lizzo wore an Old Hollywood–inspired look. She floated down the red carpet wearing a floor-length white gown with crystal trimmings, a faux fur stole on her arms, and glittering diamond rings and earrings.

Later that evening, Lizzo began her Grammy performance wearing a glittering black gown that ballooned out around her. With her musicians styled in simple black formal dresses behind her, Lizzo's dress symbolized her step forward into the spotlight. She took her time, hitting every note of her song "Cuz I Love You" perfectly, proving that her voice was as powerful as her statement gown.

As Lizzo belted out the last soul-stirring note of "Cuz I Love You," she shed her princess ball gown, revealing a futuristic-looking bodysuit with silver sparkles and flashy LED lighting. Backup dancers sprang out in matching LED bodysuits to help Lizzo perform "Truth Hurts." While Lizzo and her backup dancers swept the stage with fun dance moves, their electric energy reached the cheering people in the audience who rose to their feet.

Lizzo walked away with three Grammy Awards. She won Best Urban Contemporary Album for *Cuz I Love You*, Best Pop Solo Performance for "Truth Hurts," and Best Traditional R&B Performance for her song "Jerome." Along with her Grammy wins, Lizzo's style, performance, and natural star power let the world know that she was here to stay.

Lizzo poses with her Grammy Awards.

Truth Hurts

One of the reasons Lizzo's fans love her is that she never claims to be perfect. Lizzo never hides her struggles from the world. Yet not everyone celebrated Lizzo. As her fan base grew, so did her critics. Every week it seemed someone posted something critical about her online. Hashtags such as #LizzoisOverParty popped up all over social media.

Some called Lizzo into question for collaborating with Oprah Winfrey on a Weight Watchers campaign. When Oprah called asking to use Lizzo's song "Worship" for the campaign, Lizzo quickly said yes. But some believed that Weight Watchers was at odds with Lizzo's message about body positivity. They believed the campaign promoted the idea that thin bodies were more desirable than curvy ones. Lizzo only knew that Oprah had struggled with body acceptance just as she had. She thought that Oprah's revamping of Weight Watchers would be a great thing for women everywhere.

Criticism hurt Lizzo's feelings, but it gave her a chance to connect with her fans on a deeper level.

Lizzo listened when her critics spoke up. She took a closer look at the changes Oprah wanted to make to Weight Watchers, including incorporating ideas such as a focus on nutrition over calorie counting, an emphasis on staying active, and prioritization of self-care and mental well-being. Lizzo shared this information with her fans. Then she stressed the importance of educating others instead of shaming them. "We educate over here. We don't cancel," she said.

Lizzo faced more judgment when people began complaining that she was showing too much skin on her social media pages and in public. Many people loved Lizzo's confidence in her own skin. But others took to social media to criticize her, demanding that she cover up. Lizzo opted to ignore such critics.

By wearing miniskirts and bodysuits, Lizzo felt she was standing up against fat shaming. She aimed to show the world that bodies of all sizes can be beautiful. She knows that she's in a unique position as a celebrity and that she can use

Lizzo stays true to herself and promotes body positivity through her style.

her spotlight to demonstrate that beauty isn't one size fits all.

Cuz I Love You

On August 24, 2019, former US president Barack Obama tweeted a playlist of what he and his wife, Michelle Obama, were listening to. Lizzo's song "Juice" was no. 6 on the list. In December, Obama tweeted another list of his favorite music of 2019. "Juice" moved up to no. 4 on the new list.

People all over the world recognize Lizzo for her musical talents, her infectious laugh, and her ability to help people love all parts of themselves. But the reason why Lizzo is enjoyed by presidents, moms, kids, and more is that her music uplifts people when they're feeling down. Lizzo admits she started writing music as a way to feel better when she was sad.

Even former US president Barack Obama has Lizzo on his playlist.

By never giving up, Lizzo achieved her dreams and made a lot of amazing memories.

Not only does Lizzo's music help her feel better, but it helps her feel better about being herself. Through her music and a lot of personal growth, Lizzo has learned to love herself even when self-love and acceptance are so difficult to fully achieve.

Lizzo has never forgotten the days when it was hard to look at herself in the mirror and like the reflection staring back at her. She also remembers feeling hopeless on her darkest days. But Lizzo doesn't *want* to forget. "I think the struggle is what makes me special," Lizzo says.

After the AMAs in November 2019, Lizzo talked about

achieving huge success in the music industry: "Eight years of touring, giving out free tickets to my undersold shows, sleepless nights in my car, losing my dad & giving up on music, playing shows for free food with -32$ in my bank account, constantly writing songs, hearing 'no' but always saying 'yes' . . . Glad I never gave up."

Never giving up for Lizzo means making great music but also learning to love everything about who she is. She hopes that through her music she can pass on a message of hope and acceptance for everyone.

IMPORTANT DATES

1988	Melissa Viviane Jefferson is born in Detroit.
1997	She moves to Houston.
2000	She begins playing the flute in the sixth grade.
2005	She attends the University of Houston on a music scholarship.
2008	She plays the flute for her first real band, Ellypseas.
2010	Her father dies.
	She moves to Minneapolis.
2013	She releases her debut album, *Lizzobangers*.
2014	She and her bandmates are featured on a Prince song.
2015	She releases her album *Big Grrrl Small World*.

2016	She moves to Los Angeles.
	She releases another EP, *Coconut Oil*.
	She signs with Atlantic Records.
2017	She releases the single "Truth Hurts."
2018	"Truth Hurts" appears in the Netflix movie *Someone Great*.
2019	"Truth Hurts" reaches no. 1 on the *Billboard* charts.
	She releases her first major studio album, *Cuz I Love You*.
2020	She wins three Grammy Awards.

SOURCE NOTES

7   Alyssa Morin, "Lizzo's Insanely Tiny Purse Makes a Big Statement at the 2019 American Music Awards," E! News, November 24, 2019, https://www.eonline.com/news/1096621 /lizzo-s-insanely-tiny-purse-makes-a-big-statement-at-the-2019 -american-music-awards.

9   Jordyn Tilchen, "Lizzo Reveals She Almost Quit Music after Releasing 'Truth Hurts' in 2017," MTV News, July 25, 2019, http://www.mtv.com/news/3132710/lizzo-almost-quit-music -after-truth-hurts/.

10   Lizzo, interview by Terry Gross, "Lizzo on Feminism, Self-Love and Bringing 'Hallelujah Moments' to Stage," NPR, July 4, 2019, https://www.npr.org/2019/07/04/738474527/lizzo-on-feminism -self-love-and-bringing-hallelujah-moments-to-stage.

11–12   Phillip Picardi, "Lizzo Is the Sex-Positive, Twerking, Gospel-Singing Artist the World Needs," *Teen Vogue*, June 15, 2018, https:// www.teenvogue.com/story/lizzo-music-issue.

18   Allison P. Davis, "It's Only a Matter of Time before the World Loves Lizzo as Much as She Loves Herself," Cut, February 3, 2019, https://www.thecut.com/2019/02/lizzo-flute-pop-star.html.

21   Picardi, "Lizzo."

22   Jennifer Liu, "Lizzo Says She Almost Quit Music the Day She Released Her Now No. 1 *Billboard* Hit," CNBC, September 9, 2019, https://www.cnbc.com/2019/09/09/lizzo-almost-quit -music-the-day-she-released-her-no-1-billboard-hit.html.

24   Samantha Irby, "*Time* Entertainer of the Year: Lizzo," *Time*, accessed April 23, 2020, https://time.com/entertainer-of -the-year-2019-lizzo/.

28 Karen Gwee, "Lizzo Pulls Out All the Stops to Perform 'Truth Hurts' at BET Awards 2019," NME, June 24, 2019, https://www.nme.com/news/music/lizzo-pulls-out-all-the-stops-to-perform-truth-hurts-at-bet-awards-2019-2513407.

30 Abby Gardner, "Lizzo's Performance at the 2019 BET Awards Was So Good Even Rihanna Gave It a Standing Ovation," *Glamour*, June 24, 2019, https://www.glamour.com/story/lizzo-performance-2019-bet-awards.

36 "Lizzo Speaks on Providing Weight Watchers with Song for Rebrand," YouTube video, 59:59, posted by Snobette, December 28, 2018, https://www.youtube.com/watch?time_continue=20&tv=iHyCxVWafwA&feature=emb_logo.

38 Sandra E. Garcia, "Lizzo Wants to Build You Up," *New York Times*, September 18, 2018, https://www.nytimes.com/2018/09/18/style/lizzo-truth-hurts.html.

39 Anna Weggel, "Coffee Break: Inspiration," Current, November 26, 2019, https://www.thecurrent.org/feature/2019/11/26/coffee-break-inspiration.

SELECTED BIBLIOGRAPHY

Cooper, Leonie. "Flutes You: Lizzo and the Woodwind Renaissance." *Guardian* (US edition), July 9, 2019. https://www.theguardian.com /music/2019/jul/09/flute-lizzo-and-the-woodwind-renaissance.

Knoll, Brooke. "Lizzo's Path to Stardom Blazed by Her Flute Playing." MPR, October 16, 2019. https://www.classicalmpr.org/story /2019/10/16/lizzo-flute.

Lafuente, Cat. "The Stunning Transformation of Lizzo." *The List*. Last modified November 20, 2019. https://www.thelist.com/157551/the -stunning-transformation-of-lizzo/.

"Lizzo: 18 Facts about the Truth Hurts Star You Probably Never Knew." PopBuzz. Accessed April 28, 2020. https://www.popbuzz.com/music /features/lizzo/real-name/.

Moseley, Mariya. "Lizzo Meets 2nd-Graders behind Viral 'Truth Hurts' Video." ABC News, December 10, 2019. https://abcnews.go.com /Entertainment/lizzo-meets-2nd-graders-viral-truth-hurts-video /story?id=67628081.

Phares, Heather. "Lizzo: Artist Biography." AllMusic. Accessed April 23, 2020. https://www.allmusic.com/artist/lizzo-mn0003167672 /biography.

Respers France, Lisa. "Lizzo Treats ER Staff to Say Thank You." CNN, March 31, 2020. https://www.cnn.com/2020/03/31/entertainment /lizzo-hospital-coronavirus-trnd/index.html.

Richards, Kimberley. "Lizzo Joins Her Mom for a Sweet Dance Routine While Visiting Her Family in Detroit." HuffPost, March 3, 2020. https://www.huffpost.com/entry/lizzo-mom-dancing-detroit_n_5e5e9 7b2c5b67ed38b397735.

Rizzi, Sofia. "Lizzo the Hip-Hop Flautist Is Bringing Classical Music to New Audiences—and We're Here for It." Classic FM, December 12, 2019. https://www.classicfm.com/discover-music/instruments/flute /lizzo-hip-hop-classical-music-new-audiences/.

Spanos, Brittany. "The Joy of Lizzo." *Rolling Stone*, January 22, 2020. https://www.rollingstone.com/music/music-features/lizzo-cover -story-interview-truth-hurts-grammys-937009/.

FURTHER INFORMATION

BOOKS

Braun, Eric. *Prince: The Man, the Symbol, the Music.* Minneapolis: Lerner Publications, 2017. Music lovers will enjoy this biography of the legendary singer Prince, with whom Lizzo collaborated on the song "Boytrouble."

Levy, Joel. *Turn It Up! A Pitch-Perfect History of Music That Rocked the World.* Washington, DC: National Geographic Children's Books, 2019. Discover the history of classical, hip-hop, and other genres of music through the eyes of young people.

Zelinger, Laurie E., and Angela Martini. *A Smart Girl's Guide: Liking Herself; Even on the Bad Days.* Middleton, WI: American Girl, 2012. Learn how to practice great self-care and love your authentic self, just as Lizzo does.

WEBSITES

Girls Inc.
>   https://girlsinc.org
>   One of the original girl empowerment organizations, Girls Inc.,
>   spreads the message that girls can do anything they set their
>   minds to.

Girl Spring
>   http://www.girlspring.com
>   This website is by girls and for girls, dedicated to empowering and
>   inspiring young women.

Vevo
>   https://www.youtube.com/user/VEVO
>   Watch music videos from all of your favorite artists, including Lizzo.

INDEX